PRINCIPLES OF DIVINE PROSPERITY

How to obtain God kind of prosperity.

by:

Augustine Ayodeji Origbo

I0479757

Unless otherwise indicated, all scriptural references are from the Authorized King James Version.

Augustine Ayodeji origbo

TABLE OF CONTENT:

Augustine Ayodeji origbo

CHAPTER ONE

GOD WILL FOR ALL IS PROSPERITY

BELOVED, I WISH ABOVE ALL THING THAT THOU MAYEST PROSPER AND BE IN HEALTH, EVEN AS THY SOUL PROPERETH. (3JOHN 2)

The word prosperity simply means; all round fulfillment, overflowing satisfaction, a state of no lack, having enough to meet all needs.

When the first man was created in the Garden of Eden, he was originally created to express the likeness or similarity of the almighty God. Man was created to reason, live and behave like his creator God. God is all sufficient in nature, he never knows lack. Everything God needed in other to accomplish His project of creating the heavens, the earth and every thing in them was in God. He is called the all-sufficient God;

meaning the God that has enough to meet all need. God understand the danger of lack. He knows that when lack is present in a man life, progress will seized and fulfillment will be absent in such life. Because man is created in the image of a prosperous and fulfilled God, prosperity is therefore a 'must' for man to make his existence on earth meaningful.

The perfect understanding of the important of prosperity makes God to create the first man (Adam) and endowed him with all that he needed to be happy and fulfilled.

So God created man in his own image, in the image of God created he him; male and female created he them.

And God blessed them, and God said unto them, be fruitful, and multiply, and replenish the earth, and subdue it, and have dominion over the fish of the sea, and over the fowl of the air and over every living thing that moveth upon the earth (GEN 1:27-28).

And the lord God planted a garden eastward in Eden, and there he put the man who he had formed.

And out of the ground made the LORD God to grow every tree that is pleasant to the sight, and good for food; the tree of life also in the midst of the garden : and the tree of the knowledge of good and evil. (Gen 2:8-9)

We can clearly see from the above verses of the bible that there was no place for lack when man was originally created. Everything the first man (Adam) needed to be fulfilled was planted in the Garden of Eden. God also planted in that garden a tree of life, to keep man eternally alive and prosperous.

However, for man to continue to enjoy the prosperity of the place where he was originally placed (garden of Eden) by God, Adam and Eve (the first man and woman) must obey the instruction that God gave them to follow; this is because there are godly conditions that must be fulfill in other to have God's kind of prosperity. As it is in the case of Adam and Eve the conditions that God gave them were as follows:

And the LORD commanded the man, saying, of every tree of the garden thou mayest freely eat:

But of the tree of the knowledge of good and evil, thou shall not eat of it. For in the day that thou eatest thereof thou shall surely die. (Gen 3:6).

Adam and Eve did not fulfill God's condition they disobeyed His words or instructions. They turn away from God commandment and went ahead to eat the fruit which God commanded them not to eat.

And when the woman saw that the tree was good for food, and that it was pleasant to the eyes, and a tree to be desired to make one wise, she took the fruit therefore, and did eat, and gave also unto her husband with her, and he did eat. (Gen 3:6).

Adam and eve disobeyed their creator by eating the forbidden fruit that they were instructed not to eat. This single disobedience to God's command brought suffering, sorrow, poverty and famine to the entire human race. Instead of obeying God commands which had guarantee their enjoyment and the prosperity in the Garden of Eden where they were placed by the almighty God, Adam and Eve choose to disobey God and they brought shame to their entire descendant. God drove them from the beautiful garden of prosperity and cursed the land where they were driven for their sake.

Beloved, the common believe that some men are created to suffer while some are created to enjoy is never true, God original plan for humanity are good plan of fulfillment and prosperity. That is why God says;

For I know the thoughts that I think toward you; saith the LORD, thought of peace and not of evil to give you an expected end.(Jer29:11)

God thoughts for men are good thoughts. God delights to give men a perfect future so that his nature can reflects through them. The good thoughts that God has for men made him create a way out of the curse of poverty he had already placed on Adam and eve as a result of their disobedience in Eden. God sent his only son Jesus Christ into the world to die for the sin committed by the first man (Adam and eve), the blood of Jesus Christ that was shed at the cross of Calvary represent the blood of the first man because the wages of Adam since is death as God has pronounced on them. The moment Jesus blood was shed on the cross of Calvary the sins of Adam and it consequences transferred to Adam's descendant were totally removed. God arranged Christ death at Calvary so that the curse of poverty may be destroy and the way to God kind of prosperity and fulfillment can once again be open back to all mankind.

For the wages of sin is death, but the gift of God is eternal life (prosperous life) through Jesus Christ our lord. (Rom 6:23)

The way into life is now open to all without exception, as long as you are ready to accept Jesus Christ as your Lord and saviour, a new relationship will be restore between you and God and great doors of prosperity will follow.
In this book we shall be examining God divine principle for anyone who desire to attain God kind of prosperity in every area of their life.

CHAPTER TWO

GOD'S CONDITIONS FOR DIVINE PROSPERITY

I call heaven earth to record this day against you, that I have set before you life and death, BLESSING AND CURSING; therefore choose LIFE. That both thou and thy seed may live (Deuteronomy 30:19)

With the perfect understanding of the fact that it is God's will that every man should prosper in life, irrespective of our color or race so that God's nature can be reflected through us his creature. Let us briefly examine some vital conditions that must be fulfilled by anyone desiring God kind of prosperity or divine prosperity.

(1)YOU MUST BE BORN AGAIN.

To be born again means to be spiritually reborn. It is the spiritual transformations that take place in the life of a man when he or she accept the plan of salvation made available to all mankind by confessing and accepting the lordship of Jesus Christ.

Jesus answered and said unto him, verily, verily I say unto thee, except a man be born again, he cannot see the kingdom of God. (John 3:3)

We said in chapter one of this book that the only reason why the first man lost his chances of a prosperous life is because of sin and disobedient to God commandments. Today everyone who believe that Jesus death on the cross of Calvary represent the price that all mankind should paid to be translated or transferred back into God Eden or kingdom where prosperity abound will be   save.

This can be achieved through simple acceptance and confession. If you are not yet born again and you want to enjoy the prosperity from God then you must repeat these prayers after me;

LORD JESUS, I BELIEVE THAT YOU DIED ON THE CROSS OF CALVARY FOR MY SINS, ACCEPT ME INTO YOUR KINGDOM WHERE PEACE AND PROSPERITY ABOUND. THANK YOU JESUS FOR SAVING ME. (AMEN).

If you have said those prayers, then you have taken a very important step into enjoying God kind of prosperity. The reason for this new birth is to make all men who believe in Christ irrespective of their race, colors, or nationalities a potential candidate for success and prosperity. This also is because in God kingdom there is no sin, lack, wants, suffering or sorrow of heart.

And there shall in no wise enter into it (the kingdom of God) anything that defileth, neither whatsoever worketh abomination, or maketh a lie; but they (the born again children of God) which are written in the lamb's book of life. (Rev 21:27)

Sin is an abomination unto God, God despises sins, it defile a man, likewise is poverty an abomination unto God. Therefore, in other to be a candidate of prosperity you must like what God like and hate what God hate and obey God by accepting and confessing Jesus as your lord and saviour.

That if thou shalt confess with thy mouth the Lord Jesus, and shall believe in thine heart that God raised him from the dead, thou shall be saved

For with the heart man believeth unto righteousness; and with the mouth confession is made unto salvation.(Rom 10:9-10).

(2). YOU MUST BE READY TO OBEY GOD IN ALL THINGS

To obey God simply means to be ready to follow and keep God command without reservations. When Adam and Eve the fist mankind were established in the Garden of Eden the only thing that kept them prosperous was their obedient to God, the moment they disobey God command they fell short of God's glory and were driving out of the garden of abundance and sufficient into a place of sorrow and hard labor.

The same condition applies to anyone who wants to enjoy God kind of prosperity. God is the one who created the heaven and earth, he created the seas and all the riches in them, God knows the way to a long lasting or a never ending prosperity. For man to attain the best of God's prosperity, they must be ready to obey God at all time. They must be ready to follow his instruction no matter how foolish those instructions may look to the human eyes. Remember God ways are not men ways.

And it shall come to pass, if thou shall hearken diligently unto the voice of the LORD thy God, TO OBSERVE AND TO DO ALL HIS COMMANDMENTS WHICH I COMAND THEE THIS DAY, that the LORD will set thee on high above all nations of the earth.

And all these blessing shall come on thee, and overtake thee, IF THOU SHALT HEARKEN UNTO THE VOICE OF THE LORD THY

Blessed shall thou be in the city, and blessed shall thou be in the field. (Deu 28:1-3)

To possess the blessing and prosperity from God we must endeavour to obey and follow his words or commandments. Joshua obeyed God and became prosperous and fulfilled in God assignment for his life. God told him ahead of time:

This book of the law shall not depart out of thy mouth; but thou shall meditate therein day and night, that thou mayest observe to do according to all that is written therein; for then thou shall make thy way prosperous, and then thou shalt have good success. (Joshua 1:8).

Joshua success is traceable to his constant obedient to God word. The laws of God are the compass that leads the believers to God kind of prosperity. When we chose to disobey God's words, these will not only breach our relationship with our creator but it will also expose us to suffering and poverty because only those who obey him will have his kind of prosperity. Just as every human parent will confide more on their children who adhere and obey their commands, so will God be willing to confide his prosperity on everyone who will obey his directives. There are no two ways to divine prosperity, if you are not ready to obey God; you are as well not ready to receive from him. The scripture have this to say.

ACQUANT NOW THYSELF WITH HIM, and be at peace, thereby good shall come unto thee,

Receive, I pray thee, the LAW FROM HIS MOUTH, and lay up his words in thine heart.

If thou return to the almighty, thou shall be build up, thou shalt put away iniquity far from thy tabernacles.

Then shalt thou lay up gold as dust, and gold of opher as the stones of the brooks.

Yea, the almighty shall be thy defence, and thou shall have plenty of silver (job 22:21-25)

God still has the power to make you healthy and prosperous, however the keys are hidden in the scripture we have just read; if you acquaint yourself with him and lay his word in your heart to obey and do them you will not only swim in the rivers of God prosperity but your prosperity will also be accompanied with divine peace and good health from God.

(3) RENDER QUALITY SERVICE TO GOD

Any one who desires to be prosperous in God's kingdom must render his body to the service of the lord. When you become born again, you automatically become God's property, and as God property you must make yourself available for God's use. It is when you make yourself available for God usage that God will began to show you the way out of poverty into His kind of prosperity which are divine in nature.

If they obey and SERVE him, they shall spend their days in PROSPERITY, and their years in pleasures. (Job 36: 11)

And ye shall SERVE the LORD thy God, and he shall bless thy bread, and thy waters; and I will take sickness away from the midst of thee.

There shall nothing cast their young, nor be barren, in thy land: the number of thy days I will fulfill. (Exodus 23:25-26)

We can see from the above scriptures that God's prosperity is reserve only to those who will obey and give their life into the service of His kingdom.

Rendering serve to the lord can be done in any of the following ways;

a) It may be by talking to someone about the good-news of salvation of our Lord Jesus Christ (evangelism or soul winning).

b) by joining a service group in your local church i.e. the choir, usher or protocol, church security group, prayer and intercessory group and so on.

c). Service may also be rendered to God through given towards the necessity of the work or projects in the house of God. This also may take the form of materials or monetary gifts.

Whichever way you are led to render your body to the service of the lord, God will because of your faithfulness in service give you the key to the door of your own portion of prosperity in Him. Abraham obeyed and serves God and the lord blessed him in all things;

And the LORD said unto Abraham, get thee out of thy country, and from thy kindred; and from thy father's house, unto a land that I will shew thee;

And I will make of thee a great nation, and I will bless thee, and make thy name great: and thou shall be a blessing.

And I will bless them that bless you and I curse him that curseth thee and in thee shall all families of the earth be blessed.

So Abraham departed as the Lord had spoken unto him.(Gen12:1-4a

And Abraham was old, and well stricken in age ; and the LORD had blessed (PROSPERED)Abraham in all thing.(24:1)

Just as Abraham choose to serve the LORD and the lord prospered him, if you likewise choose to serve the lord God your creator, God will also prosper you and make your name great on the surface of the earth.

(4) DISCOVER YOU PURPOSE IN LIFE AND BE DILIGENT WITH IT.

The next condition to be fulfilled by anyone who desires to be prosperous in God is to discover his or her purpose in life and be diligent with it. To discover purpose in life means to know the reason for your existence i.e. what you are created to do or accomplish here on earth. Everyone living here on earth is created and purposed by God to accomplish different goal. If you are not doing or fulfilling your assignment here on earth, you can not experience the fullness of God prosperity. God knows everyone on the surface of the earth and He (God) commission or gave to everyman before their birth their different assignment on earth. It is therefore the duty of every Christian to seek to know through prayer from God what he or she is created to do. God is the only one that gives power for prosperity; He will not waste his resources on a man that does not know what the resources will be use for.

In other to avoid wastage, God has chosen to reveal the secret of his prosperity to those who knows their assignment on earth so that the wealth to accomplish them will be release from heaven to fulfill such assignment or purpose.

For instance, if you find yourself struggling to survive in a trade or business, if while other are progressing you are regressing, then it may be that you are not created to do such kind of business or trade. Instead of struggling to put things right in a business you are not created to do, humbly inquire from the lord for what he has destine you to be here on earth, so that His resource to make you prosperous will be release for the accomplishment of that purpose . Remember that God does not like wastage; every resource spent on a wrong purpose or a goal is a wasted resource. God said concerning prophet Jeremiah:

Before I formed thee in the belly I knew thee, and before thou comest forth out of the womb I sanctified thee, and I ordained thee a prophet unto the nations (Jer 1; 5).

God knew the prophet Jeremiah before his birth. Even while Jeremiah did not know what he was created to do, God already knew them. And Until God reveals them to Jeremiah he was not fulfill in life. Many Christian just want to do everything to prosper; if there is a call for a career in business they are there, whenever there is a call for the pulpit ministry they are also there without asking the lord opinion and if that wasn't working as they expected they will move again to another career. To them God is calling them everywhere. God is not an author of confusion he will not bless anything he did not call you to do. Beloved fulfillment and prosperity is guaranteed if purpose is discovered. Just as the secret of every product is in the hands of the manufacturer, so also is the secret of our life in the hands of God our creator. God knows everyman by name and tribe. He knows what he has created every individual on earth to be. If you ask God in prayers he will reveal to you the gap you are created to occupy here on earth and how to be celebrated in it. (GET THE AUTHOR'S BOOK ON PURPOSE IN LIFE).

Having known your purpose on earth you must be diligent with it. Stay focus to your God-given purpose or responsibility. God will not bless a lazy man. You must remain focus on what God has committed into your hands. Spend your entire life pursuing your God-given dream. It is the only yardstick to your prosperity in God. Run far away from distractions and never mind the influence of oppositions. Remember what the bible says:

Seest thou a man DILIGENT in his business (God given responsibility or purpose); he shall stand before kings; he shall not stand before mean men. (Prov22:29).

The reason why you are struggling with other over the little they have is because you have not find your own place in destiny so as to be diligent with it. Discover your God-given purpose and you will dine with kings.

(5) OPERATE THE COVENANT OF PROSPERITY

A covenant is an agreement or a contract between two people which is binding on the persons in agreement. Every party in a covenant must be committed to fulfilling their own condition for the covenant or contract so that they can all enjoy the benefits of the agreement. Any violation by any parties to the contract or of the conditions of the covenant will automatically lead to penalties or a breach in contract.

There is a covenant for prosperity and it has conditions that are attached to it in the Holy Scripture and these conditions are between man and God. It is God own portion to bless man with prosperity but it is man own obligation to obey his own portion or the conditions of the covenant of prosperity. Some of these compulsory conditions binding the covenant of prosperity is the faithfulness to the payment of tithes and offerings

TITHES AND OFFERINGS

Tithes is simply the ten percent of everyman income either material or financial income i.e. if your daily or monthly income is $1000, then the tithes for every $1000 is $100. God expressly stated in his word that anyone who refuse to pay his or her tithes is a robber or a thief, and since the curse of the lord is in the house of a thief(Zachariah 5:2-4) , the curse of the lord will be upon whatever he lays his hand to do

Will a man rob God? Yet ye have robbed me; but ye say, wherein have we robbed thee? IN TITHES AND OFFERINGS.

YE ARE CURSED WITH A CURSE: FOR YE HAVE ROBBED ME, EVEN THIS WHOLE NATION.

Bring ye all thee tithes into the storehouse that there may be meat in mine house, and prove me now herewith, saith the LORD of hosts if I will not open you the windows of heaven, and pour you out a blessing(PROSPERITY) that there shall not be room enough to receive it.

And I will rebuke the devourer for your sakes, and he shall not destroy the fruit of your ground, neither shall your vine cast her fruit before the time in the field, saith the LORD of host (MALACHI 3:8-11)

The only reason why many Christian in the body of Christ are not prosperous and fruitful is because they refuse to understand that paying tithes is 'a must'. That is tithe is compulsory for all. If you refuse to pay your tithes to God, the devil will collect it through afflictions such as sicknesses, unforeseen circumstance or problems, wrong spending, theft and so on.

Tithes are meant to be given to the priest, pastor or fulltime minister of the gospel of our lord Jesus Christ in the church of God. They are God's representative on earth. If you will not give the ten percent of your income to the pastor, priest or the ministers of God in the living church of God because you think that they are humans and not God, your door of prosperity will close and poverty will set in.

And that we should bring the first fruits of our dough (cash or currency), our offerings and the fruit of all manner of trees of wine and oil, UNTO THE PRIEST, IN THE CHAMBERS OF THE HOUSE OF OUR GOD; AND THE TITHES OF

OUR GROUND UNTO THE LEVITES (MINISTERS OF THE LORD), THAT THE SAME LEVITES MIGHT HAVE THE TITHES IN ALL CITIES OF OUR TILLAGE. (NEHEMIAH 10:37)

And all the tithe of the land, whether of the seed of the land, or of the fruit of the tree, is the LORD'S: it is holy unto the LORD.

And if a man will at all redeem ought of his tithes, he shall add thereto the fifth part thereof.

And concerning the tithes of the herd or of the flock, even of whatever passeth under the rod, tenth shall be holy unto the LORD.

And shall not search whether it be good or bad, neither shall he change it; and if he change it at all, then both it and the change thereof shall be holy; it shall not be redeemed.

These are the commandment, which the LORD commanded Moses for the children of Israel in Mount Sinai. (Numbers 27:30-34)

The doors to abundance and prosperity from heaven can only be open through your obedient to the covenant of tithing. It is a commandment and it must be obey by all.

The offerings are the free will gift given out to the service of the lord. The Offerings is also a compulsory commandment from the Lord. The only difference between the tithes and offering is that the tithes is not negotiable, it must be one tenth or ten percent of your income, but the offering is just the amount you are willing or able to avoid from your heart to give towards God's work. When you pay your tithes and offering regularly the windows of heaven will be continually open to you and you will prosper without struggling or sweat.

CHAPTER THREE

GOD'S REASON FOR DIVINE PROPERITY

God has reasons for every thing he does for his people. Prosperity is not an exception. God has very important reason for prospering everyone in the bible. This is because any thing that is void of reason will be useless in the hand of the holder. It is therefore very important for everyone who wants to have God's kind of prosperity to have a perfect knowledge of the reason why God blesses or prosper his people so that they can be eligible or qualify for it. We shall be looking at some biblical reason while God releases his prosperity on his people.

(1) KINGDOM EXPANTION.

A very important reason why God prosper his people is for the sake of expanding his kingdom i.e. for the sake of increasing the church of God.

God prosper believers so that whatever He prospers them with, they can use part of it for the support of God's work. It may be toward the need of their local church, world evangelism (printing and distribution of tracks all around the world), provision of the means of transportation to bring believers or new convert to the church premises.

Cry yet, saying thus saith the LORD of host my cities through prosperity shall yet be spread abroad; and the LORD shall yet comfort Zion, and shall yet choose Jerusalem. (Zach 1:17)

David, one of the most prosperous kings that ever lived on earth understands that God prosperity is meant only for the expansion of God kingdom. So he had it in his heart to build a house for the lord and because he has it in his heart (he understood) the lord prospered him.

And David said to Solomon, my son, as for me, it is in my mind to build an house unto the LORD my God.

Now behold, in my trouble I have prepared for the house for the LORD an hundred talent of gold, and a thousand, thousand talents of silver, and of brass and iron without weight for it in abundance; timber also and stone have I prepared; and thou mayest add thereto; (1chronicle 22;7&14)

Looking from that scripture we can see that David the king consciously prepare for the building of the house of the Lord. In our present day calculations what David gave for the building of the house of God in the Old Testament was estimated to be about twenty billion dollars ($20,000,000.000). What a man! He was totally committed to God and his kingdom.

Lay it in your heart that as from today you will give whatever God prosper you with to the support of his work in your local church and the work of evangelism all around the world. As you do this, you will begin to see great changes in your life and family.

(2) THE POOR AND THE LESS PRIVILEDGE

Another important reason why God will release his prosperity on anyone who desire them is for them to use such prosperity to take care of the poor and the less privileged in the society. God told Abraham that he will bless him and make him a blessing to others, today everyone who confesses the lord Jesus Christ automatically will receive the blessing of Abraham which are the blessing of multiplication and all-round increase. This implies that God blessing are not only for our own personal consumption but also to meet the need of others. If you are not ready to share your wealth with the poor, God will not bless you with them. Job the richest man in the whole of the east tells us the secret of his prosperity.

As I was in the days of my youth, when the SECRET OF GOD WAS UPON MY TABERNACLES (IN MY HEART);

I WAS EYES TO THE BLIND, AND FEET WAS I TO THE LAME.

I WAS A FATHER TO THE POOR; AND THE CAUSE WHICH I KNEW NOT I SEARCH OUT. (Job 29:4, 15&16)

Job explained through the above scripture to us Christian the secret to his abundance; he cared for the blind, he minister to the lame and the orphans. He advocate for those who could not avoid right justice. If anyone is ready to do like Job, then that person is ready for God kind of prosperity.

(3) FOR THE FULFILMEMT OF THE BELIEVERS DIVINE PURPOSE

Another reason why God blesses or prosper a man or a woman is for the purpose of using such prosperity to fulfill his or her God-given assignment or purpose of existence here on earth. That is why it is very important for every one to know his purpose of existence in life i.e. the area where you can occupy and be meaningful to Gods kingdom and the world around you.

If you have a pressing need for a shoe and it took you time to save a $100 bill for it. Peradventure you went into the store where shoes and other things such as cloth and necklace are sold and because of the beauty of a necklace you spent your entire $100 dollar to purchase a necklace. You will later discover that you have not actually meet your actual need and the money you have taking time to gather has been wasted on the wrong purpose. That means you may have to start saving another $100 to purchase the pair of shoe which is your pressing or actual need. Remember time and resource has already been wasted on the wrong purpose, of course It will take you another period of time and certain motivation to save another 100 dollars.

In other to avoid wastage of time and resources, God will only release his kind of prosperity on a man or a woman who understand the reasons why the prosperity are given. (Get the author book on how to discover your purpose in life)

CHAPTER FOUR

HOW TO MAINTAIN YOUR GOD-GIVEN PROPERITY.

Having examined the different condition and reason for which God kind of prosperity can be obtained. Let us briefly look into five different steps that we must take to maintain our God-given prosperity;

1) STAY FOCUS AND AVOID DISTRACTION.

In order to keep the blessings of God coming on your way. You must stay focus on what God had committed into your hand to do. Do not give room to any kind of distraction. If you loose focus of your goals and pursuit in life because of environmental or human influence, you will loose your chances of continuous prosperity.

Let thine eyes look right on, and let thine eyelids look straight before thee.

Ponder the path of thy feet, and let all thy ways be established. (Prov 4:25-26).

2) STAY PRUDENCE IN YOUR BUSINNESS

To maintain your God-given prosperity or wealth you must address every step that you take in the course of carrying out your business or goals in life, you must avoid wastage of resource, spend money only on necessity and make no unnecessary expenses that will not lead to the progress of your business. Remember, when our lord Jesus Christ multiply five loaves of bread and two little fishes, he ask his disciple to gardered the remnant so that their will be no waste. Some business men are found of abusing the blessing received from God. The moment they made unusual breakthrough or increase in their business, the next step they will take is unnecessary partying and flamboyant spending. "Now I have arrive and I am ready to show to the world that I am in business" they will say, thereby forgetting the principle and purpose for which God releases the breakthrough in the first place. If you are wasteful in nature God will collect the riches in your hand and give it to another person who will prudently use them for a godly course but if you prudently manage the little you have, you will continue to have continuous increase.

He becometh poor that dealeth with a slack hand; but the hand of the diligent maketh rich. (Prov 10:4).

A prudent man forseeth the evil, and hideth himself; but the simple pass on and are punished. (Prov 22:3).

3) ALWAYS SEEK GOD FACE OR OPINION BEFORE TAKING DECISION EITHER URGENT, SHORT OR LONG TERM DECITION.

It is a common thing among many Christian to take sudden decision in their day to day running of their life and business without seeking or finding out from God if the decisions they are taken or about to take will be fruitful. God knows the best direction you must follow to remain prosperous, after all God is the only one that can give divine ability for prosperity. Therefore in other to remain prosperous, you must cultivate the habit of seeking or asking God in prayer to instruct you on a better ideas, directions and insight e t c that will properly establish your business or life prospects. The bible talks of a king who sought the lord from his youthful age and as long as he sought the lord directions in all that he did, God prospered him.

Then all the people of Judah took Uzziah, who was sixteen years old and made him king in the room of his father Amaziah.

And he sought the LORD in the days of Zachariah, who had understanding in visions of God and AS LONG AS HE SOUGHT the LORD; GOD MADE HIM TO PROSPER (2 Chronicles 26:1&5)

King Uzziah's prosperity is traceable to his conscious effort to seeking God's direction in everything he does. He knew quite well that the way to a long lasting prosperity is only obtainable through the almighty God. He recognizes the prophetic ministry of a prophet in his reign called Zechariah who have understanding of the program and vision of God for the prosperity of his kingdom and as long as he seek directions from the lord God of Israel he remain prosperous.

Years later, when king Uzziah became great and highly prosperous, he became so proud. He felt he has accomplished so much and that there is no need to seek directions from God again. He left His role as the king and took over the priesthood office from the priest in the house of the lord. He by-pass the priest of the lord to burn incense on the altar of the lord, a job strictly met for the priest in the house of the lord. Despite all attempt to stop him, the pride of his heart could no longer allow him to obey God. He forgot that for him to remain prosperous, he need hold on to God principles and direction. As a result of his decision to do what was in his heart rather than

PRINCIPLES OF DIVINE PROSPERITY

what was in God heart, he lost his prosperous position and became a leper banished to a several house(house for the outcast) and deserted for the rest of his days.

But when he was strong. His heart was lifted up to his destruction; for he transgressed against the LORD his God, and went into the temple of the LORD to burn incense upon the alter of incense.

And Azariah the priest went in after him, and with him fourscore priest of the LORD; that were valiant men.

And they withstood Uzziah the king, and said unto him, it appertaineth not unto thee Uzziah, to burn incense unto the LORD; but the priests the sons of Aaron. That are consecrated to burn incense; go out of the sanctuary for thou has trespassed; neither shall it be for thine honour from the LORD God.

Then Uzziah was wroth, and had a censer in his hand to burn incense and while he was wroth with the priest, the leprosy even rose up in his forehead before the priest in the house of the LORD. From beside incense altar.

And Azariah the chief priest, and all the priests looked upon him, and behold he was leprous in his forehead, and they thrust him out from thence; yea, himself hasted also to go out because the LORD had smitten him.

And Uzziah the king was a leper unto the day of his death, and dwelt in a several house being a leper, for he was cut of from the house of the Lord; and Jothan his son was over the king's house judging the people of the land (2chronicles 25: 16-23).

The pride of Uzziah the king of Judah made him transgress God's commandment. Because of this act of disobedient he lost his glory to another. Any life void of God direction is heading towards destruction. If you want to remain prosperous in your God-given assignment or business then you must always seek to know

God's will concerning every decision you intend to take. God promised and also warned believers:

"I will instruct thee and teach thee in the way which thou shall go: I will guide thee with mine eye

Be ye not as the horse or as the mule, which have no understanding: whose mouth must be held in with bit and bridle; lest they come near unto thee

Psalm 32:8-9

"For I know the thoughts that I think toward you, saith the LORD, thought of peace and not of evil, to give you an expected end.(Jeremiah 29:11).

"Trust in the LORD with thine heart: and lean not unto thine own understanding

"In all thy ways acknowledge him: and he shall direct thy path. (Proverb 3:5 – 6)

There is a way which seemeth right unto a man, but the end thereof are the ways of death (Proverb 14: 12)

4) ABSTAIN FROM EVERY SINFUL ACT

Another way to maintain your God-given prosperity is to avoid any kind of sinful or illegal act. Do not be tempted into doing any bad or illegal deal that will provoke God anger on you. Remember if God is against you no man will be able to help you but if God is on your side because of your life of righteousness then who can be against you. (Rom 8:31)

Righteousness exalted a nation; but sin is a reproach to any people. (Prov 14:34)

Abstain from all appearance of evil (1 Thessalonians 5:22)

It is only the practice of righteousness that can lift up the prosperity of a man. Do not put your hands in any corruptible venture because of your desperate need of increase. Stay faithful with what God has committed into your hands and you will enjoy more increase. 'Remember he that is faithful in little much will be committed unto him'

5) REMAIN FAITHFUL TO THE COVENANT OF TITHING AND OFFERING

Anyone who wants to remain prosperous in God kingdom must continue to obey the covenant of tithing and offerings. Tithing and offerings are God keys to opening greater doors of prosperity. You must not refuse to pay your tithes. Do not say because your income or wealth has increase, therefore you can no longer give tithe or offering to God. There is no amount that is too big to give to God. Paying tithe is a commandment to all; either rich or poor, black, brown or white. Irrespective of your age, as long as you are an income earner then you must give ten percent of your income to the lord. It is the portion of the lord. Do not suspend it and do not use it alongside with your business. If you use your tithes to do business instead of given it to

God the tithes will pollute the business thereby making it a cursed business. Irrespective of the magnitude of your monthly or family expenses the tithes must not be negotiated, it must be the tenth of your income (10 percent of your income). If you do not give your tithes or offering to honour God, God in return will not honour your request for a prosperous life. Be wise. Wisdom the bible says is profitable to direct.

CHAPTER FIVE

REMAIN PROSPEROUS

Beloved, when you are created by God. God made adequate provisions for your prosperity. You are only expected to fit in yourself into God's program for your life and the great door of abundance will be open to you.

It is obedient to God's command and instructions that will guide every Christian into the path of God kind of prosperity. When you are ready to obey God in all things, every other thing will be working on their own accord for your good.

Do not hesitate to follow everything God has spoken to your heart as you read this book. You must consciously follow every step communicated through the spirit of God to you. As you take step in obeying God's laid-down rules to divine prosperity, you will live to be celebrated by all in Jesus precious name. Amen

Let us pray

ALMIGHTY FATHER, THANK YOU FOR THE
REVELATION OF THE TRUTH ABOUT HOW
TO POSSESS YOUR KIND OF PROSPERITY
MADE AVAILABLE TO EVERYONE WHO
HAVE TAKING TIME TO READ THIS BOOK.
GRANT THEM SPECIAL GRACE TO FOLLOW
THIS REQUIREMENT AND MAKE THEIR LIFE
A LIVING TESTIMONY OF A PROSPEROUS
LIFE IN JESUS PRECIOUS NAME. AMEN.

For counseling call:

00221764958083

Or write to:

Augustine Ayodeji Origbo

The word of His Grace evangelical ministry.

Bp 15577 Dk-Fann. Senegal.

e-mail: wgeministry@yahoo.fr

austine_71@hotmail.com

ABOUT THE AUTHOR

AUGUSTINE AYODEJI ORIGBO is the president and founder of The Word of His Grace Evangelical Ministry. A non denominational Christian organization whose aim is to reach the unreached and disseminate the undiluted message of our Lord Jesus Christ to the dying world through all the godly and peaceable means available. He is a teacher, Evangelist/Holy Ghost trained global intercessor and counselor of God's word. He is the author of SEVERAL CHRISTIAN AND MOTIVATIONAL BOOKS INCLUDING THE BOOK 'PURPOSE IN LIFE discovering and fulfilling it' a book specially vomited by the holy spirit to awake mankind to the reality of God divine PURPOSE and it accomplishment

www.ingramcontent.com/pod-product-compliance
Lightning Source LLC
Chambersburg PA
CBHW071143220526
45467CB00015B/1795